THE SMARTEST GUY IN THE HOOD

The Smartest Guy in the Hood

A THOUGHT-PROVOKING COLLECTIBLE SHORT STORY

Walter the Educator

Silent King Books

SILENT KING BOOKS

SKB

Copyright © 2024 by Walter the Educator

All rights reserved. No part of this book may be reproduced in any manner whatsoever without written permission except in the case of brief quotations embodied in critical articles and reviews.

First Printing, 2024

Disclaimer
This book is a literary work; the story is not about specific persons, locations, situations, and/or circumstances unless mentioned in a historical context. Any resemblance to real persons, locations, situations, and/or circumstances is coincidental. This book is for entertainment and informational purposes only. The author and publisher offer this information without warranties expressed or implied. No matter the grounds, neither the author nor the publisher will be accountable for any losses, injuries, or other damages caused by the reader's use of this book. The use of this book acknowledges an understanding and acceptance of this disclaimer.

An unsuspecting man has created a unique mathematical theorem using the principles of chemistry (proportions, stoichiometry, equilibriums, qualitative and quantitative research) to achieve extraordinary gains on the stock market. He incurs no losses and becomes one of the richest men to ever live, yet he remains living in a modest inner-city neighborhood where no one knows he has amassed a fortune.

In a small, unassuming apartment nestled within the heart of a bustling inner-city neighborhood, lived a man named Harold Retlaw. His modest home, cluttered with books, scientific journals, and scribbled notes, bore no indication of the extraordinary intellect that resided within its walls. Harold was a chemist by education and a mathematician by passion, a combination that had led him to an astonishing discovery—one that would forever alter the course of his life.

The Smartest Guy in the Hood

Harold was an enigmatic figure, a recluse who spent his days meticulously analyzing chemical reactions and their mathematical representations. He had always been fascinated by the precise nature of chemical proportions, the delicate balance of stoichiometry, and the elegant equilibrium that governed chemical processes. This fascination had driven him to ponder whether these principles could be applied beyond the confines of a laboratory.

The Smartest Guy in the Hood

One evening, as Harold was poring over his research, a serendipitous thought struck him. He wondered if the principles of chemistry, which dictated the interactions and proportions of elements, could be transposed onto the unpredictable world of the stock market. The market, after all, was a complex system of interacting variables, much like a chemical reaction. With this spark of inspiration, Harold set out on a journey to develop a mathematical theorem that would harness the principles of chemistry to predict market movements with unprecedented accuracy.

The Smartest Guy in the Hood

Harold's theorem, which he eventually named the "Stoichiometric Equilibrium Theorem" (SET), was built upon the idea that stocks could be treated as chemical elements in a reaction. By analyzing the quantitative and qualitative data of various stocks, Harold devised a formula that could predict the ideal proportions in which stocks should be combined to achieve optimal financial gains. He incorporated stoichiometric coefficients to balance the "reaction" of stock investments, ensuring that each element contributed to the overall equilibrium of the portfolio. The first step in developing SET was to gather extensive historical data on stock prices, trading volumes, and market trends. Harold painstakingly collected this data, treating each stock as an element in a vast chemical equation. He then analyzed the data using principles of quantitative research, identifying patterns and correlations that could be translated into mathematical expressions.

The Smartest Guy in the Hood

Next, Harold applied the concept of equilibrium, a fundamental principle in chemistry, to his theorem. He hypothesized that, just as chemical reactions reach a state of equilibrium where the concentrations of reactants and products remain constant, the stock market also reached points of equilibrium where the prices of stocks stabilized. By identifying these equilibrium points, Harold could predict the optimal times to buy or sell stocks, maximizing gains and minimizing losses. The qualitative aspect of Harold's research involved a deep dive into the factors that influenced stock prices. He considered variables such as company performance, economic indicators, and geopolitical events, treating them as catalysts or inhibitors in his chemical equation. By assigning qualitative values to these factors, Harold refined his theorem, making it more robust and adaptable to real-world scenarios.

The Smartest Guy in the Hood

After years of rigorous testing and refinement, Harold's theorem was complete. He began applying it to his own investments, cautiously at first, to validate its effectiveness. The results were nothing short of astonishing. Using SET, Harold consistently achieved extraordinary gains, with his investments yielding returns that defied conventional wisdom. He incurred no losses, his portfolio growing exponentially with each passing year. Despite his newfound wealth, Harold chose to remain in his modest apartment, his life unchanged in outward appearance. He continued to dress in the same worn-out clothes, shopped at the local grocery store, and frequented the neighborhood diner. His neighbors knew him as the quiet, unassuming man who always seemed lost in thought, unaware of the fortune he had amassed.

The Smartest Guy in the Hood

Harold's decision to live modestly was driven by a deep-seated belief in the value of humility and simplicity. He had no desire for the trappings of wealth, finding contentment in his intellectual pursuits and the quiet solitude of his life. Moreover, Harold understood the dangers of revealing his secret to the world. The stock market was a volatile beast, and knowledge of his theorem could disrupt the delicate equilibrium he had discovered, leading to unforeseen consequences.

The Smartest Guy in the Hood

One evening, as Harold was engrossed in his research, there was a knock at his door. He opened it to find a young woman standing there, a look of determination in her eyes. She introduced herself as Emily, a journalist from a local newspaper. Emily had heard rumors of Harold's extraordinary success in the stock market and was determined to uncover the truth. "Mr. Retlaw," she began, "I've been following your investments for some time now. Your returns are nothing short of miraculous. I believe you've discovered something extraordinary, and I want to tell your story."

The Smartest Guy in the Hood

Harold regarded her with a mixture of curiosity and caution. He had always been wary of attention, preferring to remain in the shadows. But there was something about Emily's earnestness that intrigued him. "Ms. Emily," Harold replied, "what I have discovered is indeed remarkable, but it is not something that can be easily explained or understood. The principles I have applied are complex, rooted in the intersection of chemistry and mathematics. Revealing them could have unintended consequences."

The Smartest Guy in the Hood

Emily nodded, her expression one of understanding. "I respect your desire for privacy, Mr. Retlaw. But I believe that your story could inspire others, show them the potential of interdisciplinary thinking. Perhaps we could share just a part of your journey, enough to spark curiosity and innovation without revealing the specifics of your theorem."

The Smartest Guy in the Hood

Harold considered her words carefully. He had always believed in the power of knowledge to transform lives, and perhaps sharing his story, even in a limited way, could encourage others to explore new frontiers of thought. "Very well, Ms. Emily," Harold said finally. "I will share my story with you, but we must tread carefully. The knowledge I possess is powerful, and with great power comes great responsibility."

The Smartest Guy in the Hood

Over the next few weeks, Harold recounted his journey to Emily, detailing his fascination with chemistry, his exploration of mathematical principles, and the development of his theorem. He spoke of the long hours spent poring over data, the eureka moments that punctuated his research, and the disciplined approach that had guided his investments.

The Smartest Guy in the Hood

Emily listened intently, her admiration for Harold growing with each passing day. She marveled at his modesty, his unwavering commitment to intellectual rigor, and his genuine desire to make a positive impact on the world. When the time came to write her article, Emily chose her words carefully, highlighting Harold's interdisciplinary approach and the innovative thinking that had led to his success, while keeping the specifics of his theorem shrouded in mystery.

The Smartest Guy in the Hood

The article, titled "The Alchemist of Wall Street," was published to widespread acclaim. Readers were captivated by Harold's story, inspired by the idea that seemingly disparate fields of study could converge to yield groundbreaking discoveries. The article sparked a wave of interest in interdisciplinary research, with scholars and investors alike exploring new ways to integrate knowledge from different domains. Harold, for his part, continued to live his quiet, unassuming life. He remained in his modest apartment, his fortune growing steadily as he applied his theorem to the stock market. He donated anonymously to various charitable causes, funding scholarships for promising students and supporting scientific research initiatives.

The Smartest Guy in the Hood

As the years passed, Harold's legacy grew, not as a wealthy tycoon, but as a pioneer of interdisciplinary thinking. His story became a testament to the power of curiosity, the value of humility, and the boundless potential of the human mind. And though the specifics of his theorem remained a closely guarded secret, the impact of his work reverberated through the worlds of science and finance, inspiring a new generation of thinkers to explore the uncharted territories at the intersection of knowledge.

The Smartest Guy in the Hood

In the end, Harold Retlaw achieved what few ever do—he changed the world, not through fame or fortune, but through the quiet brilliance of his mind and the unwavering integrity of his character. His theorem, the Stoichiometric Equilibrium Theorem, remained a testament to the extraordinary possibilities that arise when we dare to think beyond the conventional boundaries of our disciplines, and to the profound truth that sometimes, the most extraordinary discoveries are made by the most unassuming of individuals.

The Smartest Guy in the Hood

As Harold's reputation as a thinker grew, a subtle transformation began to ripple through his inner-city neighborhood. The local community, initially oblivious to his genius, started to take pride in the fact that such a remarkable individual lived among them. Harold's humble demeanor and unchanging lifestyle had always endeared him to his neighbors, but now there was an added layer of respect and curiosity surrounding him.

The Smartest Guy in the Hood

One day, a young man named Marcus, who lived in the apartment building across from Harold's, approached him. Marcus was a high school student with a keen interest in both chemistry and economics, having read Emily's article and been deeply inspired by Harold's story. "Mr. Retlaw," Marcus began, nervously clutching a notebook, "I've been reading about your work, and it's really inspired me. I'm trying to understand more about how you combined chemistry with mathematics to create your theorem. Could you teach me?"

The Smartest Guy in the Hood

Harold looked at Marcus, seeing in him a reflection of his younger self—full of curiosity and a burning desire to learn. He felt a pang of responsibility, recognizing the potential impact he could have on this eager young mind.

The Smartest Guy in the Hood

"Marcus, I'd be delighted to help you," Harold replied with a warm smile. "But remember, the journey of learning is a long and often arduous one. It requires patience, discipline, and a willingness to think beyond the obvious."

The Smartest Guy in the Hood

Thus began a mentorship that would last for several years. Harold tutored Marcus in the principles of chemistry, mathematics, and the delicate art of integrating the two. They spent countless hours discussing complex theories, solving intricate problems, and exploring new ideas. Harold introduced Marcus to the foundational concepts that had guided his own research, instilling in him a love for interdisciplinary thinking.

The Smartest Guy in the Hood

As Marcus's knowledge and confidence grew, he began to apply the principles he had learned to his own projects. Inspired by Harold's theorem, he developed a new model for predicting economic trends using chemical reaction kinetics. His work earned him a scholarship to a prestigious university, where he continued to push the boundaries of interdisciplinary research.

The Smartest Guy in the Hood

Meanwhile, Harold's quiet influence continued to spread. The article by Emily sparked a surge of interest in interdisciplinary approaches to problem-solving. Universities began to offer new courses and programs that encouraged students to explore the intersections of different fields. Researchers from various disciplines started collaborating, leading to groundbreaking discoveries in areas ranging from environmental science to artificial intelligence.

The Smartest Guy in the Hood

Harold's modest apartment became a hub of intellectual activity. Scholars, students, and curious minds from all over the world visited him, seeking his insights and guidance. Despite the increasing demands on his time, Harold remained true to his principles, generously sharing his knowledge while maintaining his humble lifestyle.

The Smartest Guy in the Hood

One evening, as Harold and Marcus were deep in discussion, there was another knock at the door. This time, it was a group of distinguished individuals—scientists, economists, and philanthropists—who had come to recognize Harold's contributions to the world. They presented him with an offer to fund a research institute in his name, dedicated to advancing interdisciplinary studies and fostering collaboration among the brightest minds.

The Smartest Guy in the Hood

Harold was taken aback by the offer. He had always shunned the limelight, content with his quiet life. But as he looked at the eager faces of Marcus and the others, he realized that this was an opportunity to create a lasting legacy, one that could benefit generations to come.

The Smartest Guy in the Hood

"I am honored by your offer," Harold said thoughtfully. "If we are to create this institute, it must embody the principles of humility, curiosity, and collaboration that have guided my work. It should be a place where knowledge is freely shared and where innovative thinking is encouraged."

The Smartest Guy in the Hood

The Harold Retlaw Institute for Interdisciplinary Research was established soon after, becoming a beacon of excellence in the academic world. The institute attracted top researchers and students, fostering a culture of creativity and innovation. It provided scholarships for underprivileged students, ensuring that the pursuit of knowledge was accessible to all, regardless of their background.

The Smartest Guy in the Hood

As the institute flourished, so did Harold's sense of fulfillment. He continued to mentor young minds, including Marcus, who eventually became a leading researcher at the institute. Together, they made significant advancements in various fields, their work having a profound impact on society. Despite his success, Harold's life remained remarkably unchanged. He still lived in his modest apartment, still wore his simple clothes, and still frequented the local diner. His neighbors continued to see him as the quiet, kind man who always had a smile and a word of wisdom.

The Smartest Guy in the Hood

One day, as Harold was walking through the neighborhood, he noticed a mural being painted on the side of a building. It depicted a tree with roots that extended deep into the ground, branches reaching towards the sky, and a myriad of interconnected elements—chemical symbols, mathematical equations, and various cultural motifs. At the base of the tree was a likeness of Harold, looking up with a thoughtful expression.

The mural was a tribute to Harold's legacy, a symbol of the profound impact he had made on the world. It captured the essence of his belief that knowledge is interconnected, that the pursuit of understanding transcends disciplinary boundaries, and that true wisdom lies in the ability to see the connections between seemingly disparate ideas.

The Smartest Guy in the Hood

Harold stood before the mural, reflecting on his journey. He had set out to explore the mysteries of chemistry and mathematics, never imagining that his discoveries would lead to such extraordinary outcomes. He realized that the true measure of his success was not the wealth he had amassed, but the lives he had touched, the minds he had inspired, and the legacy he had created.

The Smartest Guy in the Hood

As the sun set, casting a golden glow over the mural, Harold felt a deep sense of peace. He knew that his work would continue to inspire and guide future generations, fostering a spirit of curiosity and innovation that would transcend time.

The Smartest Guy in the Hood

In the years that followed, the Harold Retlaw Institute became a global leader in interdisciplinary research. Its scholars made groundbreaking discoveries in fields ranging from medicine to environmental science, their work driven by the principles that Harold had instilled. The institute's impact extended far beyond the academic world, influencing policy, industry, and education.

The Smartest Guy in the Hood

Harold lived to see the fruits of his labor, witnessing the profound changes his work had brought about. He continued to mentor young minds, always emphasizing the importance of humility, curiosity, and collaboration. He remained a beloved figure in his community, a living testament to the power of quiet brilliance and the enduring value of a life dedicated to knowledge and service.

The Smartest Guy in the Hood

As he approached the end of his life, Harold reflected on the journey that had brought him here. He had discovered a theorem that changed the world, but more importantly, he had inspired others to think differently, to seek connections, and to believe in the power of interdisciplinary thinking. His story was a testament to the boundless potential of the human mind and the extraordinary possibilities that arise when we dare to dream beyond the conventional boundaries of our disciplines.

The Smartest Guy in the Hood

In his final days, Harold was surrounded by those he had mentored and inspired. Marcus, now a respected scholar and leader at the institute, stood by his side, carrying forward the torch of interdisciplinary research. As Harold closed his eyes for the last time, he felt a deep sense of fulfillment, knowing that his legacy would live on in the hearts and minds of those he had touched.

The Smartest Guy in the Hood

The world remembered Harold Retlaw not as a wealthy tycoon, but as a humble genius who had unlocked the secrets of the stock market through the lens of chemistry and mathematics. His story continued to inspire generations, a shining example of what can be achieved when we dare to think differently and embrace the interconnected nature of knowledge.

The Smartest Guy in the Hood

And so, the legacy of Harold Retlaw endured, a beacon of hope and inspiration for all who seek to understand the world and make it a better place through the power of interdisciplinary thinking.

The Smartest Guy in the Hood

ABOUT THE CREATOR

Walter the Educator is one of the pseudonyms for Walter Anderson. Formally educated in Chemistry, Business, and Education, he is an educator, an author, a diverse entrepreneur, and he is the son of a disabled war veteran. "Walter the Educator" shares his time between educating and creating. He holds interests and owns several creative projects that entertain, enlighten, enhance, and educate, hoping to inspire and motivate you.

Follow, find new works, and stay up to date
with Walter the Educator™
at WaltertheEducator.com

www.ingramcontent.com/pod-product-compliance
Lightning Source LLC
LaVergne TN
LVHW051926060526
838201LV00062B/4705